Mouse-Deer Must Be Quick!

A Folk Tale from Indonesia

Retold by **Constance Foland**

Illustrated by **Joel Nakamura**

HAMPTON-BROWN

Characters

Mouse-Deer

Tiger

Tiger wants to eat
Mouse-Deer. How
will Mouse-Deer
get away?

Mouse-Deer Must Be Quick!

One day, Mouse-Deer was walking in the forest. Suddenly, Tiger jumped out from behind a tree.

"Mouse-Deer, I am going to eat you!" yelled Tiger.

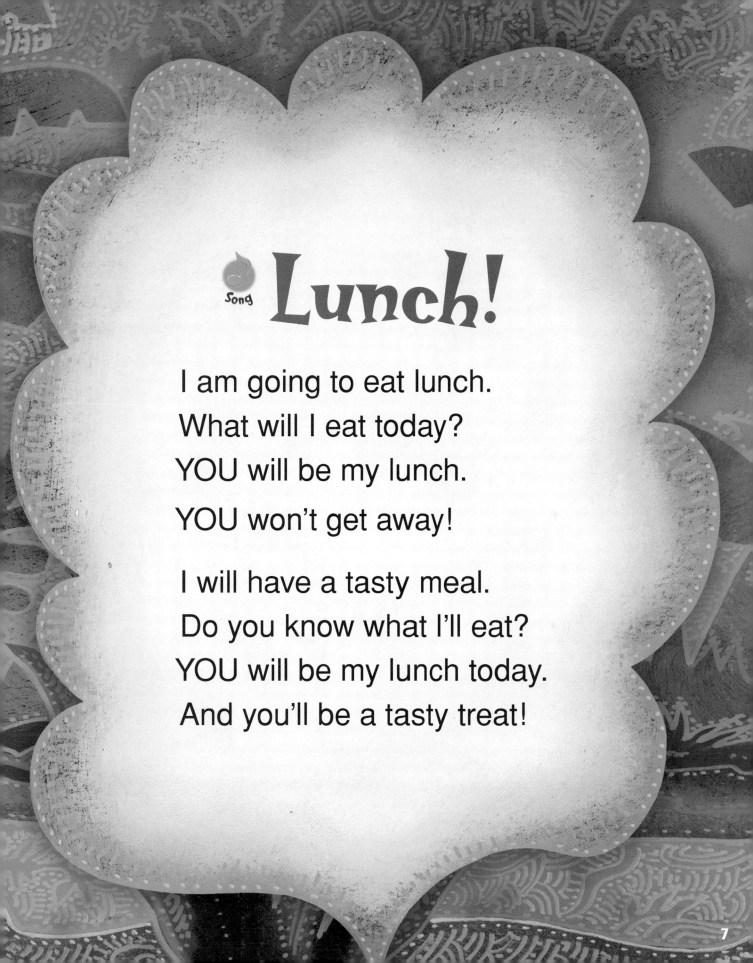

♪ *Song* Lunch!

I am going to eat lunch.
What will I eat today?
YOU will be my lunch.

YOU won't get away!

I will have a tasty meal.
Do you know what I'll eat?
YOU will be my lunch today.
And you'll be a tasty treat!

Mouse-Deer did not want to be Tiger's lunch. He thought quickly.

"You must not eat me!" Mouse-Deer said. "I am guarding the king's special cake." He pointed to a white rock.

Tiger licked his lips and said, "The king's cake must be very tasty. I would like a bite."
"No, you must not take a bite!" said Mouse-Deer. "The king would be angry."
"I will take just one bite," Tiger said.

"Then I am going to run away," said
Mouse-Deer. "The king must not see me!"
Mouse-Deer ran away and hid.

Tiger took a big bite. "OOW!" he yelled.
"This is not cake. This is a rock!"

Tiger looked and looked for Mouse-Deer, but Mouse-Deer was gone.

"Mouse-Deer!" shouted Tiger. "I will find you. I'll eat you next time!"

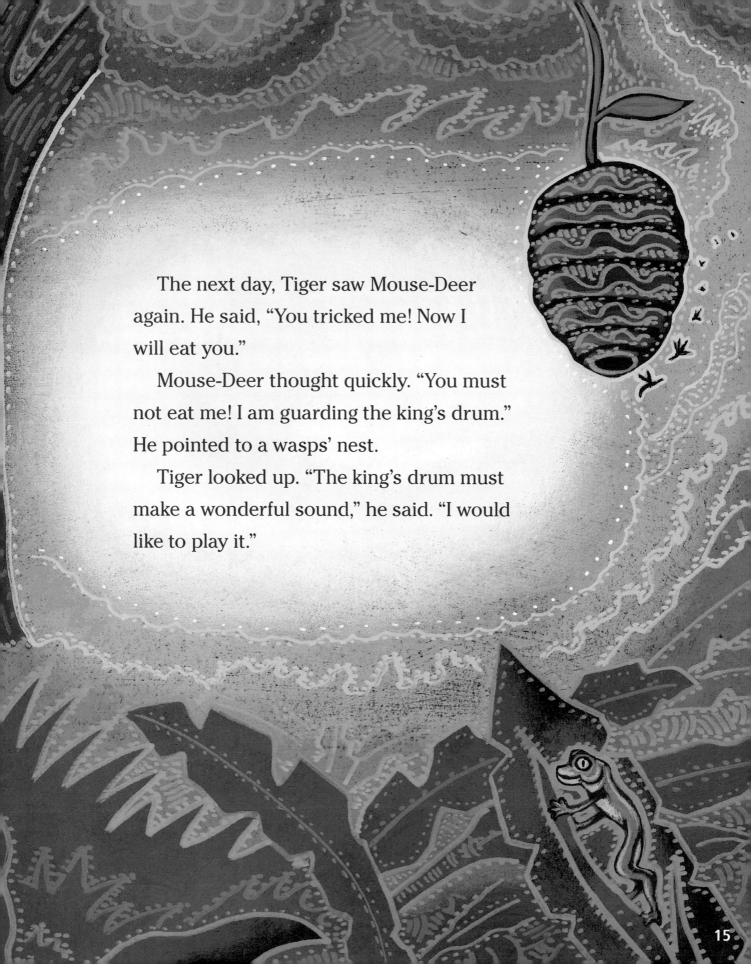

The next day, Tiger saw Mouse-Deer again. He said, "You tricked me! Now I will eat you."

Mouse-Deer thought quickly. "You must not eat me! I am guarding the king's drum." He pointed to a wasps' nest.

Tiger looked up. "The king's drum must make a wonderful sound," he said. "I would like to play it."

"You must not play the drum!" said Mouse-Deer. "The king would be angry."

"I could play it for a little while. I could play it softly. The king would not know," said Tiger.

The King's Drum

I would like to play the drum.
I would like to pound and pound.

I could play for just a while.
I could make a quiet sound.

Let me play, and you will see,
I can play so quietly!

"OK, you can play the drum quietly," said Mouse-Deer. "But first I must run away. The king must not see me!"

Mouse-Deer ran and hid.

Tiger hit the nest. BZZZZ! Angry wasps flew out and stung Tiger.

"OOW, OOW!" cried Tiger. "This is not a drum. This is a wasps' nest!"

The wasps chased Tiger. He
jumped into the river. SPLASH!

"Mouse-Deer," grumbled Tiger, "I will
find you. I'll eat you next time!"

The next day, Tiger saw Mouse-Deer again. Tiger caught Mouse-Deer and said, "You tricked me two times, but you will not trick me again. I'm going to eat you!"

Mouse-Deer was trapped!

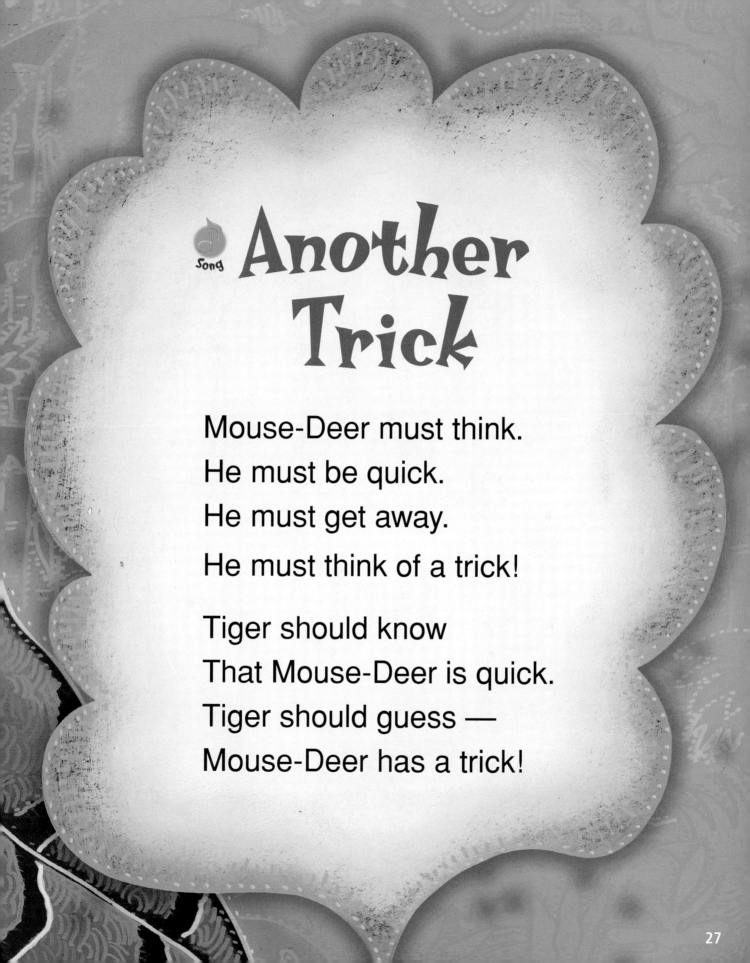

♪ Song **Another Trick**

Mouse-Deer must think.
He must be quick.
He must get away.
He must think of a trick!

Tiger should know
That Mouse-Deer is quick.
Tiger should guess —
Mouse-Deer has a trick!

Mouse-Deer thought quickly. "I am guarding the king's belt," he said. He pointed to a snake. It was asleep.

"You cannot trick me again!" said Tiger. "I will eat you now."

"You could eat me, but then this belt would not fit you," Mouse-Deer said.

Tiger thought for a moment. Then he said, "I will wear the belt first. Then I'll eat you!"

Tiger wrapped the snake around his waist. HISSS! The snake woke up. It started to squeeze Tiger.

"OOW, OOW!" cried Tiger. "This is not a belt. This is a snake! Mouse-Deer, you should help me!"

But Mouse-Deer would not
help Tiger. He just laughed and
ran away.